Christmas
DECORATING
& CRAFTS

STEPHANIE AMODIO

SNEZ FERENAC

Ro

Photographs

D1437568

The Publisher: Lone Pine Publishing

10145 – 81 Avenue   1808 B Street NW, Suite 140
Edmonton, AB, Canada T6E 1W9   Auburn, WA, USA 98001

Website: www.lonepinepublishing.com

National Library of Canada Cataloguing in Publication

Amodio, Stephanie, 1973–
    Christmas decorating and crafts / Stephanie Amodio, Snez Ferenac,
Rosa Poulin.

Includes index.
ISBN-13: 978-1-55105-448-3
ISBN-10: 1-55105-448-5

    1. Christmas decorations. 2. Handicraft. I. Ferenac, Snez, 1970–
II. Poulin, Rosa III. Title.

TT900.C4A46 2005   745.594'12   C2005-903479-3

Editorial Director: Nancy Foulds
Project Editor: Sandra Bit
Production Manager: Gene Longson
Book Design, Layout & Production: Curtis Pillipow
Cover Design: Gerry Dotto
Photography: Darwin Mulligan
Scanning: Elite Lithographers Co.

We acknowledge the financial support of the Government of Canada through the Book Publishing Industry Development Program (BPIDP) for our publishing activities.

PC: 13

TABLE OF CONTENTS

INTRODUCTION

Christmas is a magical time of year when we invite family and friends into our home to celebrate the season. Decorating the home is very personal—and with the abundance of holiday crafts, trees, ornaments, fabrics and colors available to us, it can be difficult and somewhat overwhelming to know where to begin. We recognize that there is not just one style of decorating; therefore, we have divided this book into distinct categories to help you find the right look for your home. Whether your needs are elegant, rustic, casual or something extra special for the children, it is all here. A how-to section with easy instructions and detailed pictures is included at the back of the book to show you how to make the wonderful crafts featured throughout the book.

Craft traditions can be a very significant part of Christmas. We encourage you to use the ornaments you have kept over the years and gather the children's crafts you have lovingly saved (even though the children may be adults now)—there is a place for everything! Mix new with old or traditional with modern and see where it leads you. Instead of the usual pine wreath hanging from the door, make an organza bow wreath or hang a beautiful silk bay leaf wreath. Forego the traditional tree skirt and add something special to your tree with an ultra suede tablecloth wrapped beneath. Whether you want to add a subtle hint of sparkle to your dining room or go all out and create a winter wonderland, you will be amazed at how easy it can be! Look through each section and select the color schemes best for your home—or better yet, create a color scheme completely different from anything you have done before!

In need of an updated Christmas tree? You will be delighted to find an array of ideas packed inside this book. When decorating trees, our motto is anything goes—from small, fancy shoes and fresh red roses to cowboy hats and tuxedo suits! It is not just about picking out a tree and hanging any ornament anymore; there is a definite art involved. Have you ever considered putting a Christmas tree in your kitchen or bathroom? We will show you how.

Not only is there an art to decorating the inside of the home, we also like to pay close attention to the outside. From rustic, ornamental reindeer in the backyard to elegantly lit front walkways, you will surely get your neighbors into the spirit of the season.

Entertaining at this time of year can be stressful. Our mission is to make it more relaxing and enjoyable for you. Throughout the book, there are easy tips to help make the occasion more magical. Decorate the chandelier, wrap up the dining room chairs, arrange floating candles, make table nametags, add a special floral arrangement and even end the evening with party favours. Then make sure to invite your friends and family to enjoy some of the magic!

Developing Your Ideas

Use this book as a reference for all your Christmas decorating. Use the ideas presented and incorporate your existing crafts and home décor elements. When trying to imitate an exact idea in the book, we suggest going to the following places to find similar crafts and décor items.

Craft Shows

Most cities offer annual Christmas craft shows. These shows provide excellent resources, with new trends featured each year.

Craft Supply Stores

Browsing through craft supply stores is another way to get great ideas while getting comfortable and familiar with new craft supplies.

Specialty Christmas Stores

There are stores dedicated to Christmas all year long. Watch for sales and unique items throughout the year.

Home Décor and Department Stores

There are many stunning, accessible and affordable home décor elements to be found in department stores, and we show you how to use them in unique ways.

Getting Started

Materials

Each craft in the last section of the book has a detailed list of materials you will need to make it. All the supplies you need should be available in craft supply stores. Many items you may already have on hand in your home. Carefully read each craft that you are planning to make, and then write a list of everything you will need (thus reducing the number of trips required to the craft supply store).

Setting Aside Space

Many small crafts can be created using the surface of your countertop or kitchen table. We recommend always putting a protective sheet of paper over the work surface to eliminate any accidental stains or marks. The protective paper also acts as a fast cleanup tool. Other crafts are larger and/or require hammering or the use of power tools. In these cases, we recommend setting aside a designated craft area in the basement or garage to keep the crafts confined. It may help to lay down cardboard to protect your work surface.

Safety for Small Helpers

A wonderful way to spend the holiday season is creating crafts with the help of the entire family. The last section includes a variety of crafts for different skill levels, and in most cases, we recommend the assistance of an adult—especially with the crafts that require hot glue guns, saws and hammers/nails.

In addition, a last reminder to watch all lit candles. Candles should always burn while sitting on a plate or in a flame-resistant candle holder. Never leave them unattended. If you want to move the candles after they have been burning, please wait until the hot wax has cooled and solidified.

Best wishes for the holiday season. Happy decorating!

ELEGANT CHRISTMAS

create a spectacularly
ELEGANT DINING ROOM

using crisp white and silvery blue colors. Shimmering
crystals scattered on a snowflake tablecloth pick up the
sparkle of the candles placed at each setting. Your guests
will feel quite honored to sit down on chiffon-wrapped
chairs and to receive a crystal-tied gift box. A chandelier
decorated with stunning acrylic snowflake ornaments
completes this elegant picture.

Transform your dining room into a winter wonderland; create WALL ART just for the occasion. Cover an empty wrapping paper roll with fabric or ribbon, and secure it with straight pins. Wrap and pin a feather boa around the roll. Cut thin ribbon to desired lengths and hang glittery snowflake ornaments (or other ornaments to suit your décor) from the roll.

FLOATING CANDLES create a warm ambience in any room. Beautiful beads floating beneath the water accent the star-shaped candles.

CHRISTMAS

is no longer restricted to red and green. Enjoy a pink and teal tree of elegance.

GLASS ORNAMENT TABLE NAMETAGS

Place these artistic, ornamental nametags on the table for each guest—they make memorable keepsakes for your dinner guests' Christmas trees. SEE PAGE 136 FOR INSTRUCTIONS.

PAINTED GLASS BALL ORNAMENTS

Beautifully hand-painted ornaments give a special, personal touch to your tree. SEE PAGE 132 FOR INSTRUCTIONS.

THIS ELEGANT ORNAMENT is made using an interesting twisted wire technique. String colorful glass seed beads onto thin wire, and twist the wire into a snowflake pattern. Carefully fold the wire in half to fit through the opening of a plain glass ball ornament. Lower the wire into the ornament, then delicately unfold the wire back into the snowflake pattern, using a crochet hook. Use a dab of clear silicone to hold the wire in place. You can create any pattern that you like, using one or more snowflakes of various sizes and colors.

Supplied by: TWISTED BITS OF WIRE

GIVE THE
GIFT OF MUSIC

Choose your favorite musical ornament, and place it
on a glittery gift box for the music lover in the family.

Create this unique FABRIC VASE by tucking fabric into a glass vase to cover all sides. Pick fabric to match the silk flowers. Add flair to the arrangement by skewering fresh fruit, such as limes and apples, onto bamboo skewers.

Use any canister, vase or tin bucket to assemble this lovely,

WINTRY SILK FLORAL ARRANGEMENT.

Place an oasis into the canister, and then fill with your favorite array
of silk flowers. Choose any color to complement your home décor.
Accents such as taper candles in tea light holders add a glittery final touch.

NATIVITY SCENES

A crystal nativity scene will add sophistication to any room.

This cream porcelain nativity scene, designed with straight lines and simplicity, has a modern look and feel.

Your guests will never have to sit on understated chairs again. Create this easily crafted

CONE CHAIR DECORATION.

Spray craft adhesive inside a large, plastic cone (available at craft stores). Add loose glitter and shake the cone until glitter covers the inside of the cone. Discard excess glitter. Using a single hole punch, make two holes on either side of the top edge of the cone. Pull wide organza ribbon through, then tie a knot on the outside of each hole to secure the ribbon. Embellish the outside of the cone with snowflakes or other decoration to fit your theme. Place silk poinsettias inside the cone for a final touch.

Personalize Your Family's Stockings

by transforming a plain stocking into something meaningful. Use glitter glue to write the name, and then glue a decorative ribbon on the top. Sew an ornament onto the stocking and place a picture of the person inside. Nobody will be confused as to who has been naughty or nice.

Square Glass Floral Ornament

Use ornaments in a non-traditional way. Remove the top of a square glass ornament (available at any craft store). Glue curling or gift ribbon onto all four sides of the ornament, leaving a few inches of ribbon to allow room for the rose. Tie the ribbon in a bow. Ask your florist to spray paint the edges of the rose (optional), then place it into the glass ornament, which has been filled with water. Carefully hang on your tree. Replace the roses as necessary. It does not get much more extravagant than this!

CELEBRATE the trendy designs and enjoy the new style of these decorations. It doesn't matter what your current décor is, adding different textures such as these will update your look. These decorations can also be used as hostess gifts.

STAINED GLASS CHRISTMAS BALLS

Get the children involved in making this stylish gift for their teacher.

SEE PAGE 131 FOR INSTRUCTIONS.

don't forget to decorate

YOUR BATHROOM

when company is coming. Float silk rose petals in a bathtub of water and add shimmering floating candles. Arrange candles in a variety of different colors and sizes all around the tub for romantic ambience

Introducing the Tuxedo Tree.

Make sure to keep this chic tree up on New Year's Eve for an incredible black and white affair.

We used tuxedo boxes traditionally used for wedding favors. Use glitter glue to accent the lapels. Add a feminine touch to this tuxedo tree—tie a black organza ribbon onto small, clear plastic boxes to give the impression of purse handles. Add gold beads inside for a formal flare. Gold ribbon can be elegantly tied into bow ties.

SPECTACULAR ORNAMENTS

Experiment with a broad array of spectacular ornaments in many different colors, sizes and shapes.

make your guests feel special with an

ELEGANT KITCHEN BUFFET

Arrange names on the counter (usually reserved for sit-down gatherings), and use decorative gift tags to make name tags. Wrap your silverware in black and white cloth napkins to create a two-tone effect. A gold ribbon finishes off the elegant touch. Special red-colored glasses complement the poinsettia pattern on the China dishes.

the elegance of
FATHER CHRISTMAS

Here is a fancy KISSING BALL that nobody will be able to resist. Decorate a Styrofoam ball (available in many sizes at craft stores) with fresh pine and white silk poinsettias. Traditional kissing balls are crafted from holly. We've taken the non-traditional approach by using fragrant fresh pine.

PURPLE ELEGANCE

Forego the classic colors of Christmas and delve into the unusual. Seasonal decorating is enjoyable, so have fun with colors too!

Jazz up a decorative bowl you may already have around the house with sparkly artificial fruit and glittery votive holders.

Display your pictures in an elegant photo album while entertaining.

Christmas Favors

are the perfect end to a festive evening. Fill small craft boxes with your favorite candy or chocolate and give them to your guests as they leave. Give each a personal touch by painting and gluing on accessories. Alternatively, to make dinner guests feel extra special, place Christmas favors on each plate.

Use chocolate bars in a unique way. Each bar has a special Christmas message.

Supplied by: Carrie's Chocolates & Candy Bar Wrappers

Make the evening
extraordinary by beginning with a
TOAST OF CHAMPAGNE.

Add an elegant finesse to the bathroom counter with this SMALL ANGEL TREE.

NEW YORK CHIC

Exquisite shoes from the New York Museum of Art fill this one of a kind tree.

The Pure Elegance of White

Wrapped in beautiful lace and clear lights, this tree is the perfect touch
to a cozy white bedroom.

This exquisite FEATHER WREATH is accented with a crisp white satin ribbon. Its chic look will add glamor to any room. Its versatility is endless, as it complements any color scheme.

OUTDOOR ELEGANCE

Instead of a traditional, round door wreath, hang a unique, double square wreath. Tie two Styrofoam squares (available at craft stores) together using ribbon. Cover wreaths with garlands of silk greenery, securing with floral pins. Fill in the empty spaces with silk poinsettia flowers.

CASUAL & FUN CHRISTMAS

WHIMSICAL CHRISTMAS

Use your imagination to make Christmas fun. Create a whimsical wall hanging by painting Styrofoam stars (available at craft stores) red or any vivid color scheme to suit your décor. Use Styrofoam cones wrapped in feather boas, and pin hand-made felt stockings onto a feather boa swag with clothespins. Hang a colorful ornament on a decorative picture frame and place it on the mantel. Anything goes as long as you are having fun!

Use this SILK BAY LEAF WREATH all year. Simple, classic lines make this perfect for modern living. Combine different colors and candles with distinctive scents.

FATHER CHRISTMAS STAIRCASE

THE FAMILY TREE

Photos of every family member make this tree very personal and special.
Pass this keepsake tree down from generation to generation.

PLAN A CASUAL GET TOGETHER

with friends, and have fun with it. At most
parties, guests gather in the kitchen, so
hang a festive wreath on the pantry door
and choose brightly colored serving dishes.
A glass platter of sugared fruit will give
the countertop an artistic flair.

A wonderful way to welcome your guests at the front entrance is with a SNOWMAN TREE. Use snowmen of every size and shape.

All kitchens need a pantry—so why not have a PAN-TREE? Make your kitchen fun with every kitchen ornament there is.

take pleasure in a fun and

CASUAL CARD NIGHT

in the family room. Drape vibrant fabric over the coffee table and pin sparkly tinsel around the edge. Place soft, decorative pillows on the floor to relax on. The entire family will enjoy it.

Instead of hanging a traditional wreath, use the shape of the window or pattern of the front door for inspiration. This indoor wreath smells of fresh pine.

Add uniqueness to your door swag by hanging a fresh rose centerpiece in a small vase.

Impress the neighbors with some outdoor
LIGHTS AND DECORATIONS.

Reindeer Moss
Centerpiece

Place reindeer moss in the bottom of a square glass vase. Use different shades of the same color ribbon in different thicknesses to design a grid pattern. Tie bows on top. Place flowers in the vase to see the bows on top, or place flowers higher than the bows. Tie a sheer ribbon around the vase to complete the centerpiece.

Create simple beauty in a
glass vase by layering frozen
blueberries and cranberries.

Accent your traditional garland with DECORATIVE CONES. Spray craft adhesive inside medium plastic cones (available at craft stores). Add loose glitter and shake cones until glitter covers the inside. Discard any excess glitter. Using a hole-punch, punch a hole on the top edge of the cone and pull a ribbon through it. String glass beads onto wire, and then twist around the cone. Poke a hole into the end of the cone with small pin. Thread the end of the wire through the pinhole, then twist tie to secure it. Tie cones onto a garland.

COOKIE-CUTTER CANDLEHOLDER

When planning your Christmas baking, be sure to make extras to use for this cookie candleholder. Use your favorite festive shapes when making gingerbread or sugar cookies, and then secure them to a plate with royal icing.

FRIENDSHIP FUN

Be an innovative host by creating friendship sayings on silk poinsettia leaves. Hang them on the chandelier for your guests to pull off at the end of the meal. Each of your guests will pick a silk poinsettia leaf, and then will do whatever it says. Some examples of fun sayings:

- Take a friend out for lunch
- Pick up a friend's kids after school
- Shovel a friend's sidewalk
- Take a friend to a movie
- Make dinner for a friend
- Baby-sit for a friend

Festive Fireplace

If you have an open fireplace, light it with an array of colorful candles instead of logs. As an alternative to hanging stockings on the fireplace, hang colorful tree ornaments. Greenery positioned on the mantel accents the festive swag surrounding the mirror.

ASSORTED TREE ORNAMENTS
from Pier 1 Imports

Genesis Coconut Ornament

This skilfully constructed coconut ornament has distinct beauty. Hidden within the hollow coconut is fragrant potpourri. On the inside of the lid is a Biblical quotation that matches the intricate exterior design. Make coconut chocolates and coconut soap with the leftover pulp. *Made by:* Kat n' Mouse Works

"After this I saw 4 angels standing at the 4 corners of the earth, holding back the 4 winds of the earth." Rev. 7:1

SNOWMAN DÉCOR

Count the stockings on the snowman garland, one by one.
Each day that passes, a candy cane comes out. We'll know
when it's Christmas, without a doubt!

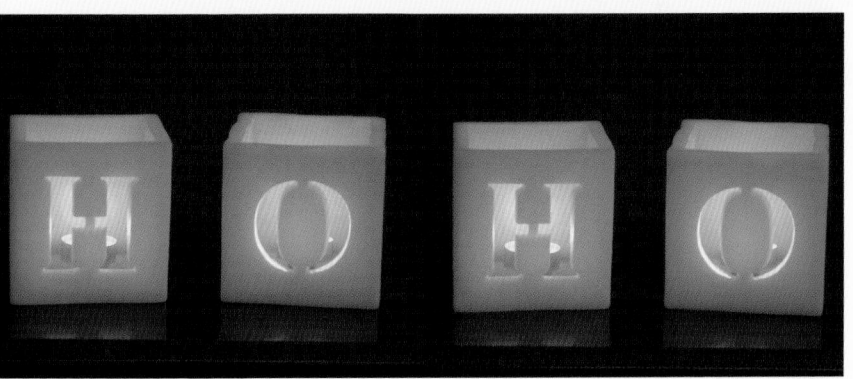

Have fun with decorative SNOWMAN CANDLES.

CHEERFUL CANDLES will brighten up your home.

This FUN AND CASUAL TABLE SETTING is anything but traditional. Use beautiful jewel-toned dishes to set the colorful mood of Christmas. Mix and match cutlery for a more casual feeling. Create simple and fun napkin holders by stringing colorful beads onto pipe cleaners and then twisting them around cloth napkins. For an interesting centerpiece, frost a glass candleholder with Crystal Creations Spray (available at craft stores), and decorate it with reindeer moss. Pinecones also add a festive touch to the table. Simply glue on colorful beads, and the pinecones come alive.

This dashing SEQUINED NUTCRACKER adds life to your décor. Christmas decorating comes alive with the brilliant colors of fuchsia, royal blue, and emerald green.

Decorate the
staircase this
season with
beautiful angels
and poinsettias.

FRONT ENTRANCE APPEAL

It's very easy to make your own swag for the front door. Gather cedar and pine branches and tie them together with a beautiful fabric ribbon. Use glittery green accents to add sparkle to the swag.

To light up your front pathway for friends, use mason jars as candleholders and place them on the steps outside the front door. Wrap the jars in ribbon to match the color scheme of the front door swag. Place the jars on fresh greenery, such as cedar or pine, to establish a warm and inviting entranceway into your home.

Your neighbors will definitely feel the spirit of Christmas when you use
FUN AND COLORFUL LIGHTS and lawn ornaments.
Do not be surprised if next year they try to out-decorate you!

RUSTIC CHRISTMAS

RUSTIC CHRISTMAS

Enjoy warm, wintry nights
with a cup of hot cocoa in
a beautiful backyard gazebo.
White lights, candles and
crafts from around the house
surround a willow tree.

Drape the fireplace mantel with a beautiful swag made of silk greenery. Use a decorative blanket instead of a traditional tree skirt around the base of the tree.

Open your home up to guests. MAKE THE VERANDA RUSTIC
and inviting by placing chairs by the door. Hang handcrafted ornaments onto
the chairs and finish the effortless look with a simple wreath.

SLED DECORATION *Made by:* NORAH SCHMOLKE

RUSTIC DINING

Bring the beauty of nature into your dining room. For the perfect centerpiece, place fresh greenery onto a luxurious ultra suede tablecloth, and add charming bird candleholders. This three tiered log candleholder completes the table; SEE PAGE 156 FOR INSTRUCTIONS. Your guests will enjoy the special additions of the small log name tag holders and the grapevine cinnamon napkin rings. SEE PAGE 157 FOR INSTRUCTIONS.

Add a touch of nature to your table with birch placemats and coasters. Cut thin pieces of birch wood around 5 cm (2") thick, then sand smooth.

As Pure and Natural as Beeswax

These beeswax candles were handcrafted with hand-dipped tapers; therefore, each one will be slightly different from the other. Pure beeswax candles are non-toxic, non-allergenic and non-carcinogenic. They burn longer than paraffin, give off more light and heat and are beneficial for people with allergies. We've used beeswax from beekeepers in Rosthern, Saskatchewan. Support your local industries by using products made close to home. For a more engaging centerpiece, wrap a wreath around the candles. *Made by:* Joan's Beeswax Candles

Accent an unadorned GREEN WREATH
with gold, organza ribbon and small, blue, ornamental balls.

Warm up an
OUTDOOR WOODEN BENCH
with a variety of wreaths, vases and greenery.

Rustic Elegance

Turn traditional rustic into urban chic. Use copper and brown tones to create an elegantly sophisticated look, and hang clusters of copper berries for added glitter. Amber feather ornaments complement the array of upscale glass ornaments. Instead of a tree skirt use a luxurious brown tablecloth.

Supplied by: THE BLOOMIN' INN

Place a DECORATIVE WREATH out front on the white snow.

Decorate a
LOG CABIN
BIRDHOUSE
and birch log birdfeeder
with pine branches and
a festive bow. Add suet to
the birch log, and watch
the woodpeckers come
all winter long. Black oil
sunflower seeds in the log
cabin will attract a variety
of birds.

Have Yourself a Merry Little Christmas

Bless this Home

GIVE THE FRONT PORCH
A WARM COUNTRY FLAIR.

SIT A CRAFTY SNOWMAN
ON A TIMBER BENCH

PAINT AND DECORATE
A GARDEN SHOVEL

LET FATHER CHRISTMAS
GREET YOUR GUESTS

A WOODEN SLED GIVES
FRONT PORCH APPREAL

Chair Décor

Dress ordinary chairs in attractive chair covers, and watch the table come to life. Gather fresh pine and attach it to the chair cover. Thread red carnations onto string, and hang them in the center of the pine. The hearty carnations will last for several days without being in water.

There are many ways to embellish kitchen chairs. Simply changing the ribbon color can modify the entire outcome of the chair décor. Hang this pinecone craft on a wall, door handle or in a window.

Instead of adding greenery to your flowers, cover the outside of a
VASE WITH PINE. Complete the unique arrangement
by securing the greenery with raffia. HINT: If your carnations are
closed, carefully brush a finger over top of each flower to open.

HANDCRAFTED REINDEER are perfect for any setting. Place them outside in a garden, on a front porch or anywhere in the house. Relocate them from year to year. SEE PAGE 150 FOR INSTRUCTIONS.

This lovely BIRD TOPIARY TREE is perfect for a home with limited space. For something fun and festive, place the tree in a natural wicker basket. Use carved wooden letters to spell out a favorite Christmas word, such as 'joy.' Add colorful pillows for a warm and inviting accent.

Handcrafted
Tree Ornaments

GLASS ORNAMENT TABLE NAME TAGS

Placing raffia inside a glass square ornament adds a rustic touch.

SEE PAGE 136 FOR INSTRUCTIONS.

CROCHET DOILY ANGEL ORNAMENT

SEE PAGE 144 FOR INSTRUCTIONS.

These homey FATHER
CHRISTMAS FIGURES
differ in style from their elegant
counterpart on page 32.

Rustic décor is completed with the final addition of a
VILLAGE SKATING RINK.

Add interest to your home with
OLD-FASHIONED CHRISTMAS DÉCOR.
Light tin trees with tea lights or battery-operated lights for added sparkle.
The vibrant color of Christmas amaryllis brings sunshine to wintry days and
looks wonderful in this silvery tin bucket.

COWBOY TREE

Decorate with Western flair, complete with cowboy boots, guns, chaps, guitars and bandannas. Conclude with a log wagon and a Western-style Santa Claus.

Neapolitan Nativity Scene

This beautifully handcrafted nativity scene was made in Naples, Italy. In 1734, Neapolitans became passionate about having a nativity scene in their homes, so small figurines began being created out of terracotta by local ceramics makers. Initially, figurines just for Mary, Joseph and baby Jesus were displayed, but soon entire villages were being made.

Each village piece, such as the lemons in this marketplace, was finished in intricate detail.

WILLOW TREE 'SHEPHERD & STABLE ANIMALS'

WILLOW TREE 'ANGEL OF WONDER'

TREE OF NATURE

Filled with woodland creatures, fishing ornaments and gardening trinkets, too, this tree will surely bring out the nature nut in you!

Rustic Christm

KIDS' CHRISTMAS

KIDS' CHRISTMAS

Make Christmas magical by decorating the children's bedroom. Waking up Christmas morning to a glowing tree draped in vibrant beads will create meaningful memories. Co-ordinate the bedding with the color theme of the room, and involve the kids in the decorating. Construct a 'Dear Santa' letter on large craft paper and have the children print whatever they wish. Be creative with other elements in the room, such as this birdcage filled with colorful ball ornaments and a feather boa. Sweet dreams.

DEAR SANTA I WANT MY LITTLE PONY DOLL TEDDY BEAR CANDY

Fun and Colorful Ornaments for the Children

SWIRLY PAINTED BALLS

Get the children involved in this mess-free, colorful Christmas craft. Using clear glass ball tree ornaments, open the top and pour different colors of paint inside. Swirl around and watch the artistic design appear before your eyes! Replace the top of the ornament after the paint has dried.

Gingerbread House

Your children's eyes will light up when decorating their own gingerbread house. Buy a prepared kit (available in grocery stores), and be sure to buy extra candies for the kids to nibble on while working. Enjoy the sweet sound of laughter as they decorate. It will not matter what the result looks like—they will love it! Capture the moment...take lots of pictures.

Teddy Bear Tree & Bedding Accessories

Children would dream to have this tree in their bedroom.

THE TEDDY BEAR HUGS
THIS TREE WITH LOVE

TEDDY BEAR WREATH
HUNG ON THE WINDOW

HAVE FUN WITH DIFFERENT
STYLES OF BEARS

Sit festive knick-knacks on the WINDOW LEDGE.

FOAM FELT FRIDGE MAGNETS

SEE PAGE 154 FOR INSTRUCTIONS.

Santa Countdown
Stocking List

1 Trucks	25
2 Dolls	24
3 Candy	23
Movies	22
	21
	20
	19

8
9
10
11 12 13 14 15 16 17 18

HANDCRAFTED SANTA CLAUS

CHRISTMAS TREES IN THE KITCHEN

The children will line up for this mouth-watering lollipop tree. Keep a jar next to the tree stocked with extra lollipops!

Gingerbread, so spicy and sweet—this GINGERBREAD TREE looks too good to eat.

Stained Glass Recipe Jar

This lovely painted glass jar makes a wonderful and meaningful gift for your child's teacher or grandparents. It includes a delicious cookie recipe with all the dry ingredients needed. Use the painted snowman again by removing it from the jar and placing it onto any glass surface.

1. Clean the inside and outside of a pickle or canning jar. 2. To outline a decorative pattern onto the jar, see instructions for the Stained Glass Window Ornaments, page 130. 3. Cut out a recipe card from construction paper. You can use the same designs as for the Gift Tags, see page 140 for instructions. Write out a desired cookie recipe (you may need to write on both sides of the card.) 4. Measure out and wrap the dry ingredients in plastic wrap and place in the jar. 5. Place a small piece of Christmas fabric over top of the jar lid and tie it into place with raffia. (You may need another set of hands to hold down the fabric while you tie the raffia.) 6. Tie the recipe card onto the jar with another piece of raffia.

SUGARED ORNAMENTS

This is the perfect craft for those in the family with a sweet tooth. Place granulated sugar into small baggies. Add different colored drops of food coloring to each bag. Close bag and shake to distribute color evenly. Spray craft adhesive inside the glass ornaments. Pour sugar into ornaments. Shake, and then discard excess sugar. Replace top of ornament.

This colorful ornament (above) was made the same way, only using rainbow sparkling sugar (available at grocery and craft stores) instead of granulated sugar and food coloring.

KIDS' CHRISTMAS TABLE

Create a fantasy table for the children's own exclusive dinner party! One look and they will feel the magic of Christmas. Wrap the kitchen table in craft paper, securing it with tape. Tie a decorative snowman bow (or other festive bow) around the table to create the illusion of a wrapped present. Draw some Christmas pictures, and then let the kids finish the coloring using special crayons with Christmas tops; SEE PAGE 138 FOR INSTRUCTIONS. Tie a basket of delicious candy onto each chair back and scatter festive chocolates on the table, just to make Christmas night even more delightful.

BELL DEER AND SANTA *Supplied by:* TRI-M NEEDLECRAFTS

Use pretty TREE ORNAMENTS
for gift nametags. It will make a special keepsake.

ADVENT CALENDAR

Fill the advent bags with their favorite candies, and the children will wake up with anticipation each day. Move a candy cane everyday for the Christmas countdown!

You will need:
- ½" (1.25 cm) red pompoms
- 20 x 24" (51–61 cm) canvas (available at craft stores)
- 25, 2½ x 3" (6.4 x 7.6 cm) cardboard bags (available in craft stores)
- green, white acrylic paint
- paint brush, pencil, red felt pen
- 1" (2.5 cm) number stencil
- 27 wooden ornaments (or decals)
- hot glue gun

Instructions:
1. Glue the pompoms onto the outside edge of the canvas. 2. Paint the cardboard bags green and white. Let paint dry completely. 3. Stencil numbers onto each bag, and then color the numbers with the red felt pen. Allow to dry. 4. Glue the wooden ornaments onto each bag, and then glue the bags onto the canvas.

'KIDS ONLY' COFFEE TABLE

Toothbrushes will have to come out after indulging in this sweets party. Tape candy canes onto wooden bamboo sticks and tie a pretty bow around to hide the tape. Place an assortment of jellybeans and lollipops into a glass vase. Randomly place the candy canes inside. Spruce up everyday paper cups with static cling window ornaments (available at craft stores). This candy vase makes a wonderful gift giving idea.

Chocolate lollipops *Supplied by:*
CARRIE'S CHOCOLATES & CANDY BAR WRAPPERS

A TREE OF YOUR OWN

All children dream of having their own Christmas tree in their bedrooms. Have them decorate it their own way—even if all the ornaments hang on one branch! Gather the home-made ornaments and all the very special ornaments given to them by family and friends. Even the personal decorations made at school can be included on this unique tree. Give your child a meaningful ornament each year (with the date on it), and this will become an honored tradition. When all the decorating is complete, the children can put their own presents under their tree.

Wooden Christmas Train

This is a perfect craft for the entire family to engage in this holiday season. The kids will be able to do most of this craft themselves, but they will need help with the glue gun.

You will need:

- natural-colored Popsicle sticks
- 20 x 30" (51 x 76 cm) foam board with blue-colored backing (available at craft stores)
- black acrylic paint
- paint brush
- thick black felt pen
- assorted watercolor paints
- ½" (1.25 cm) white pompoms
- wooden craft trees (about 2" [5 cm] in size)
- assorted shades of green-colored felt pens
- small craft Christmas presents
- colored pipe cleaners
- 2½" (6.4 cm) wooden magnetic train letters to spell out 'CHRISTMAS' (available in craft stores)
- hot glue gun

Instructions:

1. For the train track, arrange Popsicle sticks approximately ½" (1.25 cm) apart around the foam board. 2. Paint the edges and one side of each Popsicle stick black. 3. Glue the painted sticks onto the foam board. 4. Draw lines between the Popsicle sticks with the black felt pen to simulate railway ties. 5. Build a house out of the remaining Popsicle sticks, using the glue gun. 6. Paint the house with the watercolor paints. 7. Glue pompoms around bottom of house. 8. Color the wooden trees different shades of green, then randomly glue them onto the foam board. 9. Make a small igloo and snowman out of pompoms and pipe cleaners. Stick the small presents to the foam board. 10. Paint the train letters using different shades of watercolor paints and place them on the railway track.

How To

Stained Glass Window Ornaments

These colorful ornaments give a wonderful Christmas touch to windows, mirrors, glass doors or glass jars.

You will need:
- tracing paper • pencil
- large plastic bag
- DecoArt Liquid Rainbow black leading paint
- assorted DecoArt Liquid Rainbow paint colors (such as Christmas Red, Silver Pearl, Snowflake White, Dark Green and Gold Glitter)

1. Trace Christmas designs onto the tracing paper. Place the tracing paper into the plastic bag.

2. Using the black leading paint, carefully trace the patterns on top of the plastic bag. Be sure to have a constant thin stream of paint. If too much paint squirts out, you can easily wipe it off with a damp paper towel. Let stand for about 2–3 hours until completely dry.

3. Paint the patterns with desired colors. Allow to dry completely. When the paint is dry, carefully remove the patterns from the top of the plastic bag and place onto the desired surface. Hint: To achieve a transparent, stained-glass look, it is important not to use too much paint.

Stained Glass Christmas Balls

These ornaments are versatile. If the glass ball falls off the tree and breaks, carefully peel the patterns off and stick them onto another glass ball, mirror, window or glass jar.

You will need:

- paper towel • 4 glass ornament balls • ribbon
- water and vinegar solution (1 tbsp. [15 ml] vinegar to 1 cup [250 ml] water)
- DecoArt Liquid Rainbow black leading paint
- assorted DecoArt Liquid Rainbow paint colors (such as Christmas Red, Snowflake White, Dark Green and Gold Glitter)

1. Dip the paper towel into the water/vinegar solution. Wipe off the surface of the glass ornaments. Let dry.

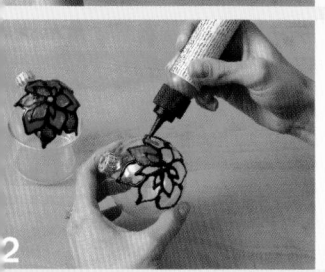

2. Using the black leading paint, carefully trace the patterns on top of the plastic bag. Be sure to have a constant thin stream of paint. If too much paint squirts out, you can easily wipe it off with a damp paper towel. Let stand for about 2–3 hours until completely dry.

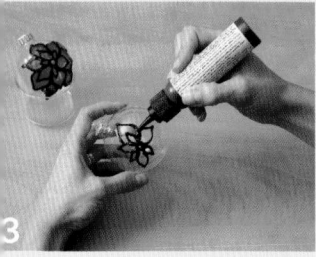

3. Paint the patterns with desired colors. Dry completely. Paint any touch-ups as needed. If any area of black leading paint is a little messy, carefully scratch it off.

Painted Glass Ball Ornaments

This craft uses paint that contains a sealant, so it is not necessary to seal the paint after the ball is painted.

You will need:

- paper towel
- water and vinegar solution
  (add 1 tbsp. [15 ml] vinegar
  to 1 cup [250 ml] water)
- frosted glass ball ornaments
- DecoArt Acrylic Enamel Ultra Gloss
  paint colors (such as Hunter Green,
  Avocado, Chocolate and Bronze)
- tin foil (for paint canvas)
- ½" (1.25 cm) angular paintbrush
- #6 filbert paintbrush

1. Dip the paper towel into the water/vinegar solution. Very gently wipe the surface of the glass ornaments. Be careful not to rub while wiping because the frosted surface will rub off easily. Let dry.

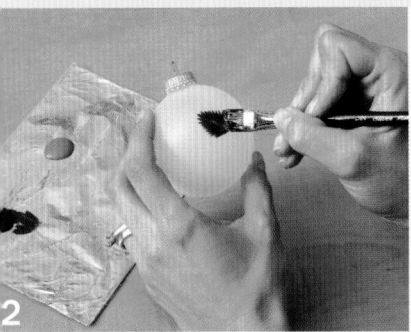

2. To paint pine branches and trees, dip the angular paintbrush into the Hunter Green. Using an upward motion, quickly lay the brush down on its angle. This will leave a line stroke of the brush. Continue this motion for the pine branches and trees.

3. Using the Avocado and continuing the same motion, paint on top of the Hunter Green, but don't cover it completely. Doing so adds highlights and depth to the pine branches and trees.

4. For the pinecones, dip the filbert paintbrush into the Chocolate paint. Using only the flat of the tip, lightly place the brush onto the glass ball to create a pinecone shape. Using Bronze, repeat the same stroke to add highlights to the pinecones. Repeat to create pattern around the ball.

Old-Fashioned Felt Christmas Ornaments

In years past, ornaments were made from materials commonly found around the house, such as fabric and yarn. These ornaments have a homemade, old-fashioned look.

You will need:

- scissors
- colored felt fabric (such as green, red, cream, purple and blue)
- cream-colored cotton string
- crafting needle
- cotton batting

1. Cut desired Christmas shapes out of felt. Remember that you need to make two of each pattern so that you can sew them together. You will need only one pattern of the accents to sew onto the front of each pattern. For example, for this tree ornament, you will need to cut out two trees and one star. Using a single stitch of string, sew the star accent onto the front of one tree. Place both pieces of the pattern together, ensuring that the sewn accent is in front, and stitch the pattern together starting from one side of the tree.

   Hint: It is easier to fill the ornament with cotton batting later if you start sewing at the side of the tree, rather than at the trunk.

2. When you have stitched around to other side of the pattern, start filling it with the batting. Keep stitching and filling with batting until all the stitching is complete.

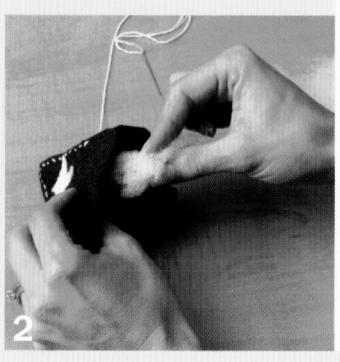

3-4. Stitch a loop of cotton string on top of the ornament for a hook. Create other felt ornaments of your own, such as a gingerbread man or mitten.

GLASS ORNAMENT TABLE NAME TAGS

Create entirely different styles by choosing diverse materials to place inside the glass ornament. SEE PAGE 12 FOR AN EXAMPLE OF AN ELEGANT ORNAMENT, or turn to page 95 to see a more rustic look. This is a nametag and a tree ornament all in one!

You will need:

- scissors
- your choice of transfer rub-on themes (with Popsicle stick)
- square glass ornaments
- stuffing material (raffia, cotton balls, ribbons)
- fabric paint (assorted colors)

1. Cut out desired transfer rub-on. Rub transfer onto glass ornament with a Popsicle stick.

2. Gently peel away transfer backing.

3. Carefully fill the inside of the glass ornament with your choice of stuffing.

4. Carefully place the top hook back onto the ornament.

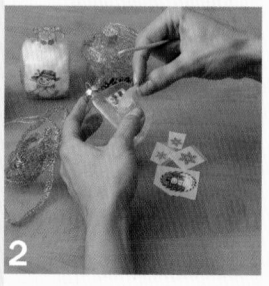

5. Using your choice of fabric paint color, write the name(s) of your dinner guests. Let dry overnight.

6. Tie the ribbon onto the hook.

Snowman Crayon Top

These wonderful crayon tops will generate smiles.

You will need:
- two ½" (1.25 cm) white pom-poms
- 1" (2.5 cm) white pom-pom
- hot glue gun
- 3 small beads
- 2 small black peppercorns
- small clove
- orange acrylic paint
- small paint brush
- scissors
- 2 small twigs, each about 1" (2.5 cm) long
- thick crayon

1. Glue the two ½" (1.25 cm) pom-poms together. Glue the 1" (2.5 cm) pom-pom on top to make a snowman figure.
2. Glue the beads onto the front of the snowman to make buttons. Glue the black peppercorns for eyes.
3. Paint the clove with the orange acrylic paint. It may take two to three coats for good coverage. Allow to dry completely. Cut off the round part of the clove from the end. Glue the cut end onto the pom-pom for the nose.
4. Glue the twigs for the arms.
5. Glue the bottom of the snowman onto the crayon.

Mistletoe Crayon Top

You will need:
- small red beads
- 2" (5.1 cm) green pom-pom
- hot glue gun
- thick crayon

1. Glue the beads onto the pom-pom to resemble a mistletoe bush.
2. Glue the green pom-pom onto the crayon.

Santa Claus Crayon Top

You will need:
- 3" (7.6 cm) red pom-pom
- scissors
- ½" (1.25 cm) white pom-pom
- hot glue gun
- 2" (5.1 cm) white pom-pom
- 1" (2.5 cm) white pom-pom
- 1 large bead
- 3 small beads
- thick crayon

1. For Santa's hat, cut the red pom-pom into the shape of a tree. Glue the ½" (1.25 cm) white pom-pom onto the top of the red pom-pom.
2. Glue the bottom of the red pom-pom onto the 2" (5.1 cm) white pom-pom (Santa's face).
3. For Santa's beard, cut the 1" (2.5 cm) white pom-pom into a slight 'V' and then glue onto the bottom of the 2" (5.1 cm) white pom-pom. The point of the 'V' should be on the bottom.
4. Glue on the large bead for the nose.
5. Glue on the 3 small beads for the eyes and mouth, and then glue to the top of the crayon.

Christmas Tree Crayon Top

You will need:
- 3" (7.6 cm) green pom-pom
- scissors
- small beads
- hot glue gun
- thick crayon

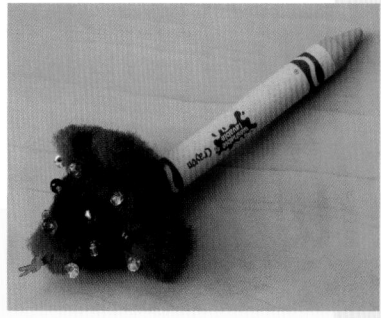

1. Cut the green pom-pom into a tree shape, starting from the bottom going up into a point.
2. Glue the beads onto the pom-pom to resemble tree ornaments. Glue a bead on top of the tree for a star.
3. Glue the bottom of the pom-pom onto the crayon.

Gift Tags

No need to spend money on gift tags anymore.
Re-use old Christmas cards from last year, and
give them a personal touch.

You will need:
- old/used Christmas cards
- decorative paper scissors
- assortment of colored construction
  paper
- glue stick
- twine
- ½" (1.25 cm) single hole punch

1. Cut desired images out of the Christmas
   cards using the decorative scissors.

2. Glue images onto the construction paper.
   Be creative with the type of scissors and
   the angles you use.

3. Write a note on the front or back of the
   tag. It is now ready to place on a wrapped
   present.

1-4. The following gift tag is made the same way as the tag on the previous page, except you add a string to tie the tag to your present.

5. Punch a hole in the top corner of the finished tag. Cut a piece of twine approximately 10" (25 cm) long, and pull it through the hole. Glue or tie it onto your wrapped Christmas present.

SNOWFLAKE GIFT WRAP

Add a personal touch to a wrapped present by creating this beautiful snowflake imprint on top.

You will need:

- paper
- scissors
- small pieces of sponge
- acrylic paints (in colors of your choice)
- ceramic tile or tin foil to use as a paint palette
- packaged gift

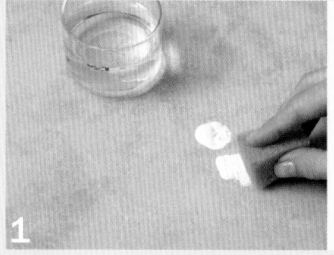

1. Fold and cut the paper into a snowflake pattern. Place pattern onto wrapped gift. Alternately, use masking tape to hold the pattern in place.

2. Dip the sponge into the desired color of paint. Sponge the color onto the top of the snowflake pattern, making sure to sponge all the cut out pieces.

3. Carefully remove the snowflake pattern and let the paint dry.

   Hint: Before removing the snowflake pattern, sprinkle glitter onto the paint before it dries.

1-3. This snowflake design is an alternative to the snowflake gift wrap. Simply sponge the snowflake design (as shown on the previous page) onto a piece of white paper using a paint color that matches the wrapping paper. Cut out the snowflake with decorative scissors and glue onto the gift wrap.

CROCHET DOILY ANGEL

You will need:

- 6" (15 cm) round, white doily
- 1½" (3.8 cm) pearl-colored, tin ornament ball
- scissors
- hot glue gun
- white, artificial poinsettia (with gold trimming)
- Spanish moss
- artificial greenery and berries
- black permanent marker

SEE PAGE 95.

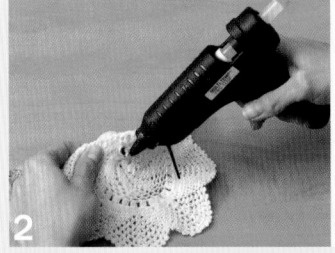

1-2. Lay the doily flat. Fold the top of the doily over to about the middle, then turn it over. Cut the wire off the pearl ball. Ensure that the metal end where the wire came from is still intact. Push the metal end into the doily for the angel's head. Glue the metal end to the doily.

3. Fold the sides of the doily inward to create a triangle.

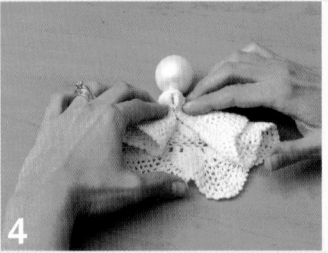

4. Glue the top and in between the folds of the triangle onto the metal end of the ball.

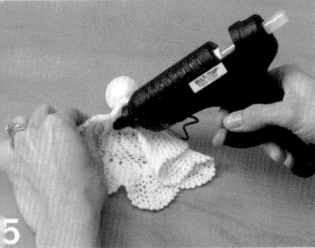

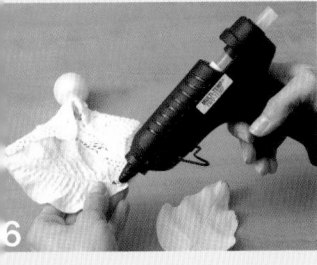

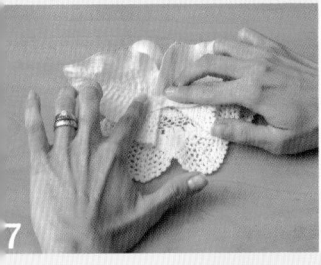

5. Make sure to glue the top folds to the metal end to ensure that the metal end is covered and not showing.

6. Cut two of the biggest petals from the white poinsettia and glue them onto the back of the doily (where the folds show) for wings.

7. Ensure that the tips of the poinsettia leaves are facing upwards and that they are overlapping each other when glued onto the back.

8. Glue the moss onto the top of the tin ball for the angel's hair. Trim the hair once it is glued so that the hair is neatly groomed around the angel's face.

9. Glue artificial berries on the front of the angel's dress.

10. Make a wreath for the angel's head with the artificial greenery and berries.

11. Draw the eyes, nose and mouth with a permanent black marker.

Hint: To add rosy cheeks, brush on some blush or pink eye shadow.

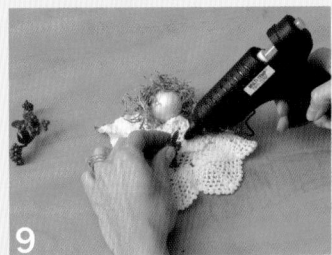

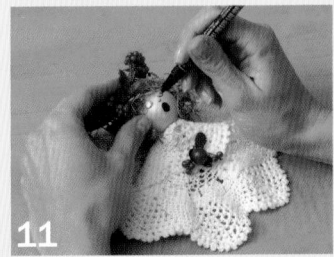

Welcome Sign

Hang this sign outside for your family and friends to admire.

You will need:

- fine sand paper
- wood (your choice of shape)
- all-purpose sealer
- flat paint brush
- DecoArt Acrylic paints (such as Uniform Blue and Titanium White)
- round dry paint brush #12
- hand drill
- freshly cut wood twigs (green and brown in color)
- pruning scissors
- 3 long branches
- ½" (1.25 cm) nails
- hammer
- duct tape
- hot glue gun
- old/used toothbrush
- 19 gauge wire (black or green)
- wire cutters
- artificial pine branches, pine cone

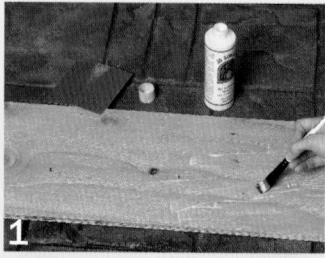

1. Sand the wood. Paint the entire piece of wood with the sealer. When dry, lightly sand again to remove any air bubbles.

2. Paint the front and all sides with Uniform Blue paint (may require 2 or 3 coats). Allow to dry completely between coats.

3. Dry-brush the Titanium White over the blue paint to create a snowy look. Drill a hole at the top end of the wood. Hint: Before dry-brushing, and once the paint is on the brush, brush in a back and forth motion on a piece of paper first to make the paint dry.

4. Cut the green twigs into the sizes needed to make the tree trunks and branches. Cut the brown twigs into the sizes needed to spell out 'WELCOME'. Nail all the twig pieces to the wood.

5. Flatten nails that protrude out the back.

6. Cover nails with duct tape to protect your work surface and hanging surface.

Finishing Touches

· Cut thinner pieces of the brown twigs into four pieces for the stars. Glue these onto the wood and on top of each other.
· Water down some Titanium White and mix it using the toothbrush; then, use the toothbrush to splatter the paint onto the wood. This technique creates a snowy winter look. Work in a con- fined space, such as a box, to prevent flying paint from staining your walls, floor or furniture.
· Wire together the three long branches, leaving about 12" (30 cm) of wire on either end. Attach the wired branches through the two holes that were drilled earlier. Wire the two ends together, integrating the pine branches and pine cone into position on either end of the branches.

Hint: Be careful not to flick the bristles too much or too quickly when splattering the paint across the wood.

Birdhouse Wall Hanging

This is the perfect craft for all seasons.

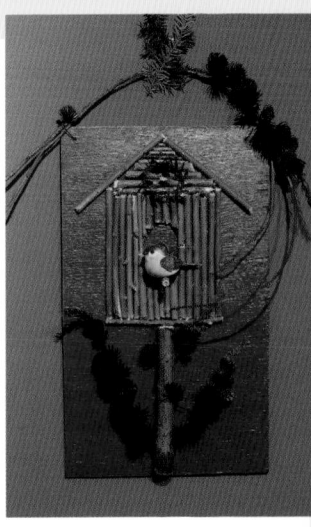

You will need:

- plywood or any smooth wood, cut to the desired size
- drill • hammer
- ⅛" (63 mm) wood drill bit
- medium sandpaper
- all-purpose sealant
- flat, size 12 paintbrush
- DecoArt acrylic paints (such as Victorian Blue and Winter Blue)
- round dry paintbrush #12
- garden snips
- 2" (5.1 cm) nails
- ¾" (1.9 cm) nails
- hot glue gun
- artificial pine greenery
- artificial pine cones
- artificial berries
- artificial bird
- artificial green moss
- floral green wire
- wire cutters
- duct tape
- twigs (one thick twig for holding bird house; two longer, thin twigs for hanging; one short, thin twig to form the entrance of the birdhouse; several medium-sized twigs for creating the walls of the bird house) Hint: Use freshly cut twigs if possible, because they are more pliable and easier to work with.

1. Drill two holes in the upper corners of the wood piece about ½" (1.25 cm) from the edges.
2. Sand and paint surface with 2 coats of sealant. Then paint with Victorian Blue.
3. Use the garden snips to cut the thick twig to the desired length for the branch to support the birdhouse.
4. Form a circle with the short, thin twig to make the entrance of the birdhouse.
5. Cut a 2" (5.1 cm) length of the medium-sized twig, and glue it about 1" (2.5 cm) below the entrance to create a perch.
6. Paint the blue-painted surface only (including the entrance to the birdhouse) with the sealant. Form branches on the thick twig with lengths of the artificial pine greenery and glue into place. Glue artificial pines into desired locations on branches.
7. Create a wreath using the artificial branch and berries. Glue the wreath onto the center of the roof. Glue green moss onto the bottom of the entrance of the birdhouse. Glue artificial bird onto the perch.
8. Follow the hanging instructions of the Welcome Sign on page 147.

GARLAND OF BEADS

Be as creative as the abundance of colors and sizes of wooden beads available.

You will need:

- heavy-duty natural color jute twine (at least .078" or 2 mm in diameter)
- assortment of multicolored wooden beads
- scissors • Scotch Tape

Hint: Make certain that the holes in the beads are only slightly larger than the diameter of your twine. You want knots in the twine to hold the beads in place.

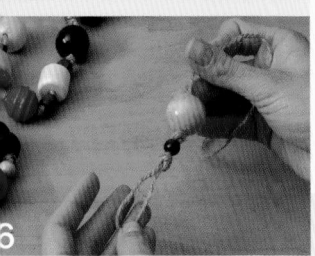

1-4. Cut the desired length of twine to make the garland.

Hint: The finished length will be slightly shorter owing to the knots required to keep the beads in place. Starting 8" (20 cm) from one end of the twine, make a loop knot for hanging the garland.

5. At the other end of the twine, tightly wrap a small piece of Scotch Tape to allow the beads to thread easily onto the twine. Start by threading a small bead onto the tape/twine, and pulling it to the knot.

6. Make another loose knot as close as possible to the end of the bead. Thread a larger bead onto the twine and tie another loose knot at the end of the bead. Continue this alternating pattern.

Hint: Alternate colors and sizes, or create your own pattern. Stop about 8" (20 cm) from the end of the twine. Tie a loop knot with the remaining twine.

Wooden Reindeer

We used wood from poplar trees to make these decorative reindeer.

You will need:

- chop saw (or radial arm saw)
- hand drill
- ½" (1.25 cm) drill bit
- 1/32" (0.79 mm) drill bit
- hot glue gun
- 5, 1½" (3.8 cm) nails
- 6, 3" (7.6 cm) wood dowels ½" (1.25 cm) in diameter
- large piece of wood for body, about 5" (13 cm) wide and 12" (30 cm) long diameter
- 2 medium pieces of wood for head and tail, about 4" (10 cm) wide and 6" (15 cm) long
- 4 small pieces of wood for legs about 2½" (6.4 cm) wide and 12" (30 cm) long
- 1 small piece of wood for neck, about 2" (5.1 cm) wide and 4" (10 cm) long
- 2 small pieces of wood for eyes, about 2" (5.1 cm) wide and ½" (1.25 cm) thick
- 2 small twigs for antlers (use twigs with many branchlets)

Decorations:

- 1" (2.5 cm) artificial red berry for nose
- wreath for neck

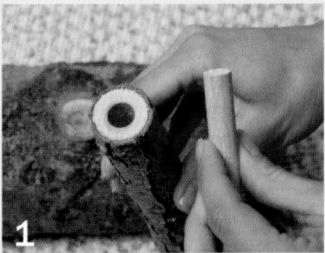

1. Drill five holes at the desired angles with the ½" (1.25 cm) drill bit, about ½" (1.25 cm) into the body for the four legs and neck. Cut the legs and neck pieces at this same angle.

2. Drill a ½" (1.25 cm) deep hole into the top of each leg and into both ends of the neck piece using the ½" (1.25 cm) drill bit, and insert dowels into each hole.

3. Insert the legs and neck into the body. Using an approximate 5° angle, shave the front portion of the head piece on two sides, leaving about 1½" (3.8 cm) unshaved along the 6" (15 cm) length of wood. Keep the two shavings for the ears. Drill a 1½" (3.8 cm) deep hole into the bottom of the head piece at the desired angle. Shave the other medium piece of wood to form a tail.

4. Pre-drill a small hole into the tail piece using the ⅟₃₂" (0.79 mm) drill bit, and attach the tail to the rear of the body using a nail.

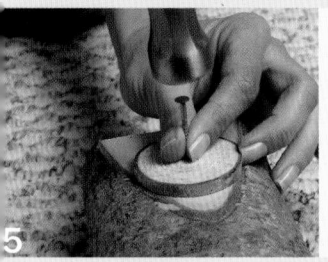

5. Saw two 2" (5.1 cm) pieces of the wood for the eyes. Pre-drill a small hole into the ear and eye pieces using the 1/32" (0.79 mm) drill bit.

6. Attach the ears to the rear of head piece. Attach the eyes to the shaved off areas on either side of the head.

7-11. Drill two ½" (1.25 cm) deep holes at the desired angle using the ⅟₃₂" (0.79 mm) drill bit. The diameter of these holes should match that of the antler twigs in front of the ears. Place a decorative wreath around the neck of the reindeer. Attach the head to the neck. Insert the antlers, using glue to make sure that they are secure. Attach the berry for the nose.

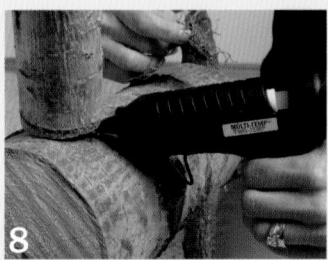

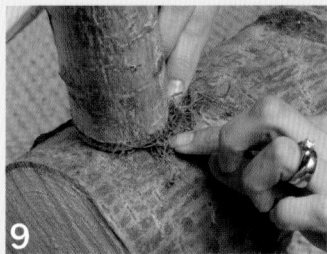

CHRISTMAS CRACKERS

Homemade Christmas crackers will add a personal touch to your Christmas dinner table. Make one for each family member and/or guest at the table.

You will need:
- small piece of paper, 1" (2.5 cm) x 2" (5.1 cm)
- pen • cracker strip • 1 string of raffia
- toys/gifts
- homemade tissue paper crown (see below for instructions)
- toilet paper roll or wrapping paper roll cut into 5" (13 cm) lengths
- 6 x 11" (15 x 28 cm) homemade wrapping paper, made from packing paper
- hot glue gun

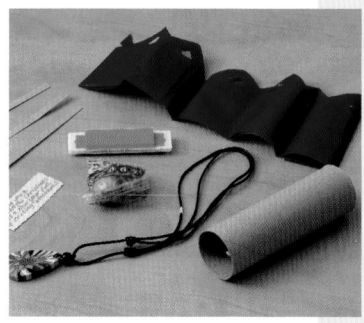

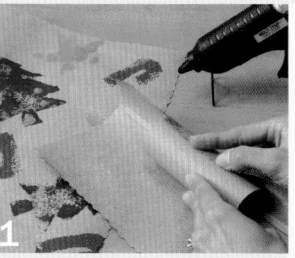

1. Write a fortune on the small piece of paper and place it, the gifts and the paper crown into the paper roll. Place the roll on top of the wrapping paper and roll the wrapping paper over the tube. Glue the wrapping paper to the roll and then to itself so that it does not come apart. Hold for a few seconds so that the hot glue adheres to the wrapping paper.

2. Wrap (do not tie) the raffia onto one end of the wrapped roll. Carefully tighten the raffia so that it leaves an indentation on the roll. Do not over tighten the raffia or it might rip through the paper. Remove the raffia and repeat at the other end. This will give the roll a crimped/tied look. If the prizes are falling out through the crimped ends, repeat and pull the raffia a bit tighter. Ensure that the cracker strip is showing through both ends of the wrapped tube. Decorate each cracker with greenery, berries or images cut from recycled Christmas cards. Use crafting scissors to make unique and interesting cuts.

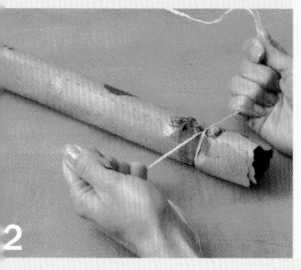

HOMEMADE TISSUE PAPER CROWNS

Cut tissue paper lengthwise into 1" (10 cm) strips. Cut triangular shapes along one edge of each strip to represent jewels. Fold the two ends over each other and tape together.

FOAM FELT FRIDGE MAGNETS

These colorful magnets will add a festive touch to your bare fridge. You can even make these magnets into brooches or attach them to wrapped presents for an added gift giving idea.

CHRISTMAS TREE

You will need:

- tracing paper • pencil
- green foam felt • yellow foam felt
- scissors
- hot glue gun
- miniature craft string of tree lights
- magnetic tape

1. Trace a tree pattern lightly onto the green foam felt.
2. Trace a star pattern lightly onto the yellow foam felt. Cut out both patterns.
3. Glue the yellow star onto the top of the tree.
4. Glue on the string of tree lights. Carefully glue the strings to the back of the foam.
5. Cut a 4" (10 cm) long piece of magnetic tape and stick to the back of the tree.

HOLLY

You will need:

- tracing paper
- pencil
- green foam felt
- scissors
- hot glue gun
- 3 red 1" (2.5 cm) pom-poms
- magnetic tape

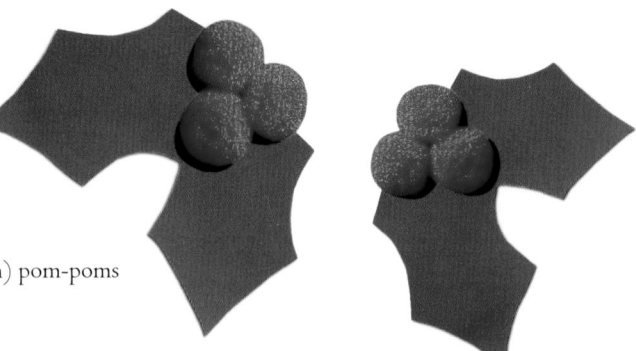

1. Trace two holly leaf patterns onto the foam felt. 2. Cut out both leaves, and glue them together at the base of the leaves. 3. Glue the red pom-poms onto the base of the leaves. 4. Cut two pieces of magnetic tape about 2" (5.1 cm) long, and stick them to the backs of the leaves.

Hint: If you do not have red pom-poms, cut three 1" (2.5 cm) circles out of red foam felt, and glue them onto the base of the leaves.

Snowman

You will need:

- tracing paper • pencil
- white foam felt
- black foam felt
- scissors
- red or orange foam felt
- brown pipe cleaner
- ½" (1.25 cm) single hole punch
- 3 pieces of ribbon, two 2" (5.1 cm) long and one 4" (10 cm) long
- 2 small beads of your choice
- magnetic tape

1. Trace a snowman and hat pattern lightly onto the white and black foam felt. Glue hat to head.
2. Cut out a nose from the orange felt, and hole punch the black felt for eyes and buttons. Glue on.
3. Glue the 4" (10 cm) ribbon across the neck. Glue it onto the back of the foam felt. Glue one of the 2" (5.1 cm) ribbons under the last ribbon. Glue the last piece of ribbon on top of the first ribbon and fold over the top piece. Trim the ends of the two ribbons.
4. Cut the pipe cleaner into two 3" (7.6 cm) pieces, and glue them to the back of the foam felt over top of the glued ribbon. These are the arms. Cut two 1" (2.5 cm) pieces of the pipe cleaner and twist onto arms to create fingers.
5. Cut two pieces of magnetic tape 1½" (3.8 cm) and 2½" (6.4 cm) long and stick them to the back of snowman.

Star

You will need:

- tracing paper
- pencil
- yellow foam felt
- scissors
- hot glue gun
- magnetic tape

1. Trace a star pattern lightly onto foam felt, and cut it out. 2. Cut a 1" (2.5 cm) piece of magnetic tape, and stick it onto the back of the star.

Three Tiered Log Candle Holder

Rustic candle holders make for a warm, country setting. SEE ALSO PAGES 80–81.

You will need:

- 3 logs of different widths and lengths, see instructions below
- burlap twine
- glass votive holder
- I candle
- 3 artificial holly leaves
- artificial berries
- hot glue gun
- I small 3" (7.6 cm) wide grapevine wreath
- 2" (5.1 cm) saw tooth bit
- 3 artificial small eggs
- artificial green moss
- radial arm saw
- drill press

1. Using the radial arm saw, carefully cut logs into the following sizes. The first log should be the thickest at about 3" (7.6 cm) wide by 11" (28 cm) long. The second log should be a bit thinner at about. 2½" (6.4 cm) wide by 9" (23 cm) long. The third should be the smallest at about 1½" (3.8 cm) wide by 7" (18 cm) long.

2. Using the drill press, carefully drill a 1½" (3.8 cm) deep, round hole into the top of first (widest) log.

3. Chisel any pieces of wood that are rough.

4. Arrange all three logs so that they are all touching each other in a close fit. Using the burlap twine, tightly wrap the twine around all three logs, making about eight to ten rotations. You may need someone to hold the logs in position as you wrap. Tie the twine off into a knot, leaving the ends a little long.

5. Using the hot glue gun, glue on the artificial holly leaves and berries. Glue the artificial green moss along the rim on the top of the widest log into which you drilled a hole.

6. Place the glass votive into the drilled hole. Place a candle into the glass votive.

7. Glue the small grapevine wreath on top of the second widest log. Glue some artificial green moss into the middle to create a nest. Glue the three artificial eggs into the middle of the nest.

Grapevine Cinnamon Napkin Ring

These napkin rings do not take much time at all to make, and they make a natural addition to a rustic table. SEE ALSO PAGES 80–81.

You will need:
- hot glue gun
- artificial greenery (pines and berries)
- wire cutters
- 3" (7.6 cm) round grapevine wreath
- natural raffia
- 3 cinnamon sticks

1. Glue the greenery onto one side of the wreath.
2. Glue twisted raffia onto the greenery.
3. Break the cinnamon sticks into three desired lengths, and glue them onto the raffia and greenery.

Small Log Name Tag Holders

The final addition to a rustic dinner table.

You will need:
- table saw
- small wooden logs
- artificial pine branches • artificial berries
- assortment of colored construction paper
- decorative paper scissors
- glue stick • twine rope
- metallic colored pens

1. Using a table saw, cut small wooden logs into 5" (13 cm) pieces.
2. With the table saw, create a ¼" (63 mm) deep groove down the middle of each wood piece. Use caution when handling small pieces of wood on the table saw.
3. Glue the artificial pine branches and berries onto the fronts of the wooden logs.
4. Cut the construction paper into 4" x 2" (10 x 5.1 cm) sections using the decorative paper scissors. Write names on the paper using metallic colored pens.

Acknowledgments

Thank you to the following merchants who allowed us to use props for our photo shoots: Blyss Décor, Mikasa Home Store, Pier 1 Imports, Rafters Home Store, Stokes (South Common), Flower Affairs and Flowers on 50th.

A very special thank you to the following families who graciously opened their homes to us for our photo shoots:

Carlo and Lina Amodio

Anne and Rajko Boras

Connie Edwards

The Henderson Family

Maryann Lahure

Harvey and RoseAnne Lawton

Christine Lund

Penny MacInnis

May and Norm Prokopchuk

Susan Scarfe

Glen Shepherd

Author Biographies

Stephanie Amodio merges her home economics background with her experience in publishing. As owner of Stephanie Amodio Consulting, she specializes in project management, writing, editing, proofreading and marketing and promotions. She has contributed to more than 75 books and magazines published in Canada and the United States. For this book, Stephanie served as project manager and principal author.

Snez Ferenac has capitalized on her natural flair for decorating by opening her own design business, Distinctive Design. She helps people accessorize their homes, designs party décor, serves as a personal shopper and designs gift baskets for any occasion. She has been prop styling for five years on various cookbook projects, creating beautiful tablescapes to showcase delectable food. Snez served as set designer and prop stylist for all the crafts displayed in this book.

Rosa Poulin's inspiration and support in creating new ideas for crafts come from her loving husband, Michael, and their wonderful daughter, Zina. This is the second Lone Pine Publishing craft book Rosa Poulin has been involved with, the first being the very successful *Halloween Recipes & Crafts*. Rosa created and assembled many of the crafts featured in this book.

INDEX OF CRAFTS

Numbers in bold indicate instructions in the How To section.